Eat My Words
one bite at a time

by Arthur Weil

Eat My Words
one bite at a time

Copyright 2010 by Arthur Weil.

All rights reserved. No part of this book may be reproduced in any form except for the inclusion of brief quotations in a review or article, without written permission from the author.

For all inquiries or to order additional copies of this book, contact Arthur Weil, 208 Pala Avenue, Piedmont, CA 94611, by email at: aweil444@aol.com or go to www.poetrypearls.com.

These books make excellent gifts and are autographed by the author.

Pricing is $4.95 per copy.

ISBN: 0-9788456-5-x
Printed in the USA by United Graphics Incorporated

Acknowledgements

Working with Arthur Weil has been a source of great inspiration. He has boundless energy and generosity and is full of thrilling stories. He has endless poetic creativity pouring from his fingertips. As an incredibly young octegenarian, he gives his written work a sense of timelessness and sagacity well beyond his years. This, his 17th book, brims with poems and sayings that can be appreciated by all. I do hope you find as much enjoyment in Arthur's writings as I.

Alison Bodden

Other titles by Arthur Weil:

Dare-Devilish and Divine
Have Fun While You Can
Words to Fly With
Life, Love and Gems That Shine
Exploding Mind (or 'Not Over the Hill Yet')
Poetry is for Sissies
Reflections of the Moment
The Fluid Word
Slice of Life
Theater of Thoughts
Love Always
Liquid Words
Not Shakespeare, Just Me
Wacky and Wonderful, Wireless Words
Word Missiles, Here and Now

Please visit me at my website:
www.poetrypearls.com
blog: http://arthurweilpoetry.blogspot.com/
or look me upon Facebook!

TABLE OF CONTENTS

Explore	6	Wisdom	27
Good Intentions	7	Flashes Of Childhood I	28
Amazing Day	7	Leaving Footprints	29
April Fool	8	Flashes Of Childhood II	30
Somebody	8	Teen Advice	32
You've Got It	8	You Are Not God	34
Once In A While Stop	10	I Would Judge	33
Sunlight	11	Half Asleep	35
Possibilities	12	Meditative Thought	36
For You	12	I Do What I Can	37
Creative Brain	13	Let The World In	38
A Miracle	14	Wringing Out The Mind	39
Split/Sliced	15	Control	40
Get To Know Her	17	Learners	41
Words Touched	18	Aspire	42
Stages Of Life	19	King On The Mountain	42
Never Too Late	20	Innocence Of Youth	43
Spins On Its Axis	20	A Spit In The Ocean	44
Threshold Of The Universe	22	Dare Me	46
Celebrate	23	Rain	48
You Can Make It	23	Price Tag	49
Poetic License	24	Topple The King	49
A Bit Of Quiet	25	We March	50
Reward Myself	26	Victory In Defeat	52

Closeness	53	Getting Ahead	76
Buzzbomb	54	Peace	77
An Ode To My Pen	56	Proprietary Information	77
Just Happiness	58	Create A Climate of Happiness	78
Listen! Listen!	60	Generosity	78
Care For The Brain	61	Funky People	79
Cashmere Sweater	61	Advice For Teenagers	80
Challenge Adversity	62	Crowd	81
Age And Youth	63	Friendship	81
Ecstatic Energy	64	How High is High?	82
I Fiddle My Day Away	65	Doors	83
Ego To Feed	66	Lieselotte	84
Can I Share This With You?	67	Dessert	86
In My Own Backyard	68	Evaporate	87
It's Never Too Late	68	Flowers	88
Bury The Hatchet	69	Daily Task	89
Mental Teen Dance	70	Time	90
Forget	71	Banana	91
Competitive Drive	71	Believe	91
Mr. Good And Mrs. Mean	72	Just For Today	92
Walk With Grace	73	Drugs and Alcohol	93
Who Are We Really?	74	Distractions	94
Rebirth	75	Power of Words	95
Watch It Grow	75	A New Year Wish	96
What Makes Me Tick?	76	Let Me In	96

Some people can never admit
They can ever make a mistake
It's always someone else's fault

Someday they will graduate from Kindergarten

EXPLORE

It's natural to socialize
If friends were clever, just a little wise
Some dumb, some nice, some smarty
All out for crazy fun and party

We rap, listen to music, text
Do goofy stuff, not knowing what's next
Some gals and guys do explore
One or the other wants some more

"It all depends, I want to stay friends"
Just say "No, not ever, not now"
We're curious, and don't know how

Aren't you a teenager and not so sure?
Being grounded, chewed out's not the only cure.

*Sing me a song of
healing and solace
And I sing one of hope
Torn out of my
inner soul*

*Why go to school
when you can Google?*

*There's joy in sun
And blooming flower
And all that lives each precious hour
Time to love flies and fleeting
What is gone is not repeating
Do not wait - you know how
So share, enjoy each moment NOW!*

*All of us have our inner child
Let us out - go crazy wild
Usually full of duty obligation
Quite OK to join the silly station
And dance, laugh and cheer
So much healthier than fear*

GOOD INTENTIONS

On this day
In my way
Did I help the poor
Did I take time to listen
Did I improve the world one iota more
Did I show and share love
Did I uplift or was I uplifted
My human touch to those less gifted
Did I study, read and learn
Lose my inhibitions, hope and yearn
Did I repay my bets or debts
Oh, wondrous day
Before I fall asleep
Wish me, protect me
Good intentions I must keep

Lift up your spirits
Run away from negatives
And learn to laugh more

Everything has its price,
especially if it's free

AMAZING DAY

There isn't a silent second
That adds up to
A silent minute
Which adds up to be a noisy hour
And a fantastic, symphonic
Colorful,
Spectacular day

All to return
To the still blackness
Of the night

Life is to live and love and share
It is to feast, to do, and care
So thank you,
For your greatest wealth
Is friendship and the best of health

APRIL FOOL

Please press my humor button
I can't seem to reach it

Keep your cool
It's an April fool
Spring has sprung
The lark has sung
You simply hold your tongue

> The train ever moving
> Brings us new vistas
> Never to return
>
> Enjoy the ride...

April fool
Sit on the stool
You've got one ear of a different size
Glance down and you may realize
Your body's not yet ready for a prize

April fool
The year just ended has but started
Ice cold, frozen drift has parted
The hope of spring
Reborn, rejuvenated, new does optimism bring

April fool
With hope and sun
Hopeful predictions frolic fun
Yet share with school, with duty and with work
Yet time for courting, loving vibrant is our perk

April fool
All is just make-believe
My parents' nagging mellowed to reprieve
If I can only win the race, catch a ball or join the chase
I'll know I am lucky in the phase

SOMEBODY

I felt I was nobody
I know that is not true
For you are dear and here
That makes an even two

YOU'VE GOT IT!

Talent to spare
Talent to care
To demonstrate
Or new shape create

You've got it!

Oh, I envy such creatures
Who display gifted features
Be they athletes, artists or scientists
We adore, cherish them always be missed

You've got it!

Geniuses produce new medicine
Invent tools to keep our water clean
Compose new musical tunes
Make the young maiden swoon

You've got it!

Or demonstrate Olympic fate
Open new venues, opportunity's gate
On pedestals these greater leaders
Greatest authors for us readers

You've got it!

Witness great philosophers explain or warn
Geneticists invent new grains and corn
And yet all of us have talents too
We shape tomorrow's society, me and you

You've got it!

No rioting, no fuss
There is a gift and talent in all of us
Go, climb the ladder to your success
Takes diligence, hard work to truly now confess

You've got it!

*This is the most communicative generation;
cell phones, computers,
sometimes we even speak at the dining table*

ONCE IN A WHILE STOP

once in a while
stop what you do
stop

stop
close your eyes   reflect
open up your spirit and your intellect
seek truth
in silent meditation
nirvana one step nearer
put the world aside
emotions mushroomed with elation
like onion skin
the levels peel
newness   revealed
thankful   transformed
you'll feel
deep breath
slow   slowly   more rest
continue back to doing
new adventure   challenge brewing
know
life will be different from now on

open to new ideas

> *The unspoken is often
> the most powerful*

*Life, joy is yours and mine
Wish luck and good health
A bit of effort we'll do fine
So go to it!*

SUNLIGHT

In small shapes I see
hues and many colors - green
Each so distinct, each so pristine
lemon, purple, pineapple,
tomato, pear, tangerine and orange
strawberry succulent
Yet it's the bright sun's glow
often penetrating the leaves
leaving the many mottled shadows
the symmetry of cloud and light
all green
moving in the wind
now seen
with my own eyes
my own world

POSSIBILITIES

The world isn't all
That it's cracked up to be

A world of opportunities for all time
An infinite universe of possibilities

If you call putting a triangle
Into a square hole
Possibilities

It all depends on the open door
Who walks through it
And what did they do
With the hole in the doughnut?

Life is an exciting constant puzzle
Don't despair
You'll make it
Possibilities

Don't fake it, don't take it
Don't break it
If you do
God forsake it

Always respect Mother Nature;
She has a fiendish sense of humor

FOR YOU

I welcome you
With love and open arms

Much is primitive, simple, diluted
Polluted

Just to read
To nurture the mind
For that I love and thank you

Some of my rhymes may touch
A raw nerve
Some interactive
Some close and dear
Evoke a smile, a chuckle or a tear

I love and thank you
You are the winner

Internalize
Feel like the winner of a special prize

Joyous, exploratory
Adventurous beginner

*I hear the airplane above
But I intend to sit pretty in
the here and now*

Weil's dog Bella

CREATIVE BRAIN…

now neutral   lame

fatigued, exhausted

too much, too fast   to blame

yet we live asleep and latent
     the myriads of strands

         in cells
       that we call brain

we live   sustain
                      G
                      O
                      D
                      S

magic brain computer
simply turns neuter

rest, reflex, reborn
         my brain soon will blow
it's horn

soon restore   pinnacles   of extradition
just patience until I reclaim

my new born will

Careful!   Use it.
   It's all up there - those grey cells
     To lead,   to share
The miracle of the brain's calculating fibers
It's yours to keep,   to treasure

But only for a time

A MIRACLE

A sprightly, beautiful girl
Creeps constantly into my thoughts
While I dress, eat, study,
Am I obsessed?
At silent moments
Wonder what she thinks?
What would she say?

I see her face, her profile
Her smile, her composition
"I miss you!"
The echo of her voice
Cuts through the class
Stifles the noise
Consumes my thoughts

I text
She reciprocates - cheerful
"What did U do today?"
So we do encourage
The buzzing sparks at both ends
Abundant smiles and compliments
Exultation - adoration

A craving for nearness, togetherness
When do we see each other next?
What shall we do together?
Where to eat, where to hang out?
Where to share in silence and closeness?

This new grand feeling
Two sweethearts
A miracle - wrought by heaven
Lived and devoured
A craving for much more!

Please don't tell!

SPLIT/SLICED

Split, sliced
Pulled in every direction
Torn, confused, frustrated
What next? What now?
Why me?
Divisive, ignominious
I want to leave
Get out of here - go
The shrill of the phone
Guilt, commands
Lists incomplete
A prisoner in my own body
Collapse, numb
I'm not me anymore
But that's OK
Batteries can be recharged
Mine can too!

>   This is for you: take it or leave it
>   But please do read it
>   Bit by bit
>   It may
>   just
>   fit

> *Vacations are to restore balance and energy,*
> *not to burn it up exhaustingly,*
> *ready for another vacation*

In nature, man is an animal, to be tamed but not enslaved

> *The fickle finger of fate*
> *Like lightning strikes again*

When we step into the elevator we push the right button
But when we open our mouths we forget to do the same

> *One friendly, cuddly pooch*
> *Can make you feel*
> *Better than most indifferent people around you*

I said something stupid
And I know it
I wonder if the stupid listener
Understood how stupid it was?

>You can sweep your fears under the rug
>But they will always crawl back to haunt you

If you stop running, amazing things will happen
If you would only listen and look

>Brilliant ideas are like stars,
>If we could only harness their energy

The bright sun bends through my window shades,
Muted with enough diffused light for me to think

A gorgeous, sunny, cloudless day
A whisper of a breeze
In front of my window, barely a stir
I sit mesmerized, thinking
How lucky I am
More day is still ahead of me

>I hate to clean up
>Especially my mess
>But there comes a time
>When I face my own maturity

Youth looks ahead
Elders - at the past instead
Perspective and a point of view
Old or young wish it were true

Berkeley Repertory Theater Gala 2010

GET TO KNOW HER

She's a tomboy
Full of muscle, springy and bright
Such a delight
Get to know her, you'll be thrilled
All your fears and apparition stilled

Just like you so full of zest
Each exciting hour face the test
Know, adore
Find out and explore
She's so much more

She's so much more

*I got all excited about this
special day
I may even get out of bed*

WORDS TOUCHED

So much to share and tell!
Some ideas fabricated - others I know well
But you, dear reader,
Can turn the page any time!
Toss my book, or lap up every line
Or erase me out of your mind
And go routinely as you are - missed out and blind
You, teen reader, are creative; do not need kings
You can combat the vegetation and
the nothingness of things!
Or pry open your heart
And pour your feelings onto the doorstep of time

*At the beach I saw the endless horizon
which leads to eternity,
But I am still here*

STAGES OF LIFE

The babe's head purple, struggling
Flesh torn born
Into a challenging world
Each stage in life
The heavens and the earth unfurled

Why curious, conscious
Brief innocence helpless

Defensive   excessive   cautious
Always learning   absorbing   questioning
Mating   binding   nurturing   family and friends
Growing   knowing
Optimism   realism   new directions

Extroversion and introspection
You wonderful, wonderful world

It is through knowing pain that joy enthralls
It is failure that brings hope, driving force
Out of the mean new value our goodness and success
It is through silent, lowly prayers
Infallible or rational belief, in spirit's awe
So blessed

We grow, mature
Excited on life's tour.

Reach high - the light will lead
Enjoy each day
Life passes by with speed

If I knew then what I know now
I'd know I ran into a dumb old cow

NEVER TOO LATE

Never too late to tolerate
With kindness put up with
Those you hate
Dull your thought
Your feelings overwrought
Each of us destined to our fate
No choice
But learn to live and tolerate
Or leave this world
Fend off the feelings of the enemy's hate,
Before it is too late
Lest you too become infected, so destructive
Like your adversary

Live life,
Partake with friends
Pursue your dream of satisfaction
Good food, lots of love and action
Squash the hatred
Celebrate!

It's not easy
A great challenge!

SPINS ON ITS AXIS

As the world revolves
So too our tumultuous life
Spins on
Its own axis
Helplessly
We spin with it
Barely keeping our balance
Don't you feel it?

Better to venture
Do it now
Than soon forget
And not know how

Do alarm clocks ring
To wake you up
Or to make you guilty
And ruin your day?

Is the 13th day a superstition
Good or bad, it's your decision
If there were no calendar and we didn't know
You'd act the same - on goes the show

Benny Bufano mosaic, Oakland, CA

THRESHOLD OF THE UNIVERSE

With visions and fireworks
Pinnacle on Mount Loneliness
I experience the hues of the rainbow
Frothing, haunting formation of clouds
Cirrus, Nimbus - like angels, scaring demons in the sky
The radiance, the magnificence of life
Uncanny inspiration, all too short!

You and I stand at the threshold of this universe
Confined, deliberate - ready to dare or do
Planted firmly to explore our vision
Gift of life in all its brilliance

Like Moses holding the tablet of the Ten Commandments
Downward - exhorting his people
To abandon the Golden Calf
So you too - here - retreat from the steep mountain
Inspired/halo - visionary
Truth - in awe of The Creator,
The Unifier of the Universe

Queen/King of nature's power

Admire, thankful, humble
In this, our place, the infinite universe
The spirit is within you - me!
Yet, we are but on the threshold!

Go, take another first step!

We often are the wayward stranger
Ready to discover the inner self
As we seek joy, contentment and love

CELEBRATE

Live life, partake with family and friends
Pursue your dream of satisfaction
Good food, lots of love and action
Squash the hatred, envy jealousy
Celebrate!

It's not easy.
A great challenge!
Never too late

Strip away all things
And material possessions
See the greatness of
The real you!

YOU CAN MAKE IT

He who says "You'll never make it"
Be astute, evaluate
You can take it

Diligent in fortitude
Study, plan
Your interlude
You conceive your plan
Because you can

Learn, practice
Go, it's yours to do
Your action, your belief

Do not forsake
Unless you really try
You'll never know if you can make it
Earn your share of the pie

Caesarea Amphitheater, Israel

POETIC LICENSE

(the flexibility used by a writer to heighten the effect of their work. May include exaggerations)

Poetic license can go a long way
Even to sundown's horizon
Dawning revelations
A touch of infinity; careful phrasing

Do not overstep!

A torrent of lovesick declarations
If only we secretly could share
The glue of love with our radiance
You with me, I with you - that's true

A heap of trouble once printed out
No place to hide once exposed
The power of the word
Has defeated many a giant.

Careful - less you ignite humanity
Foster change
And want a statue
Named after you

A BIT OF QUIET

Sometimes

In this tumultuous time
    A bit of quiet,
      Silence,
        Is just fine
          No radio,
          Stereo,
           Computer
           Or TV

  Just
I   on   I
A world of me
And as you sit,
Silently contemplating
An endless world of ideas,

Picture the real you within
  Soul   and   heart

    Sit

Like Buddha
On a space of nothing,

Soon,

    Your eyes closed,
      But your mind alert
        You may
          Relive
            The best of your
  past
            Or perhaps
              The best
                Of your
  future

REWARD MYSELF

This cookie buttery laced is my treat
New computer, gigantic 3D TV can't be beat
New shoes, clothes, gadgets of every kind
Accolades, congratulations - simply now I find

You ridicule, you cast a hiss
Don't give a damn, lick or kiss
Most critical of me, so full of doubt
To you my life a failure a bad route

Yet I, so victorious like Hercules could move boulders
Success, smile, pat myself (with pride) on both shoulders
Dexterous, with elegance I prance on air
'Cause I feel proud, I made it care

Smile now from cheek to cheek
With dancing heart at eagle's peak
I find myself, I finish what I started
I added, helped, see fruition not yet parted

Compliments, handshakes in life's upper atmosphere, so rare
Highly motivated, simply chart my way, pay my own fare
I'm busy, self-content and of the happy, grouchy sort
For mine the world, the pinnacle, horizon on my own accord

I owe you the world and you owe me
I used you and you used me you see
From clay and elements with a touch of life
I've bounced, consumed rip roaring rife

So what, so when, so now that counts
The dance of death far distant haunts
Join me who made it in a thousand ways
Let us love and live in great unison until the end of days

Regardless of obstacles, we sing our own song every morning, in tune or not...

WISDOM…

Is in sharing the best of your
Experience
Chuckling at your past
Mistakes, imperfections
Knowing
Life is in flux
There is always something
New to try

Most of us have to learn
By failure, experience
The hard way
Time the healer and destroyer
Will whisper
Doubt
Your inner sanctity
Will feel the unsure answer
Is wisdom knowing better
Or to omit judging the impossible

So what? A bit bashful, sure!
With understanding comes the cure
If I am shy or hesitant, it's OK
I will survive, feel better the next day
For sometimes it is best not to know
To admit mistakes, ignorance
Shed arrogance, replace by humility
Know your day will come in the end

FLASHES OF CHILDHOOD I

Flashes of childhood: licorice, raspberries
Pungent smell of red, ripe apples
Climb the pear tree
Bite into the rich, ripe juiciness
Sugary fluid dancing over my cheek

From there, the grandeur spy in awe
Wide vistas of green-yellow meadows
Nearby, a burbling, crystal clear brook
Glistening like a snake, meandering
Cascading, rippling like a deer at play
Past worn-out barns, past dilapidated farmhouses
Lush green, licking the moist riverbank

The song of a mating game
Distinct croak of frogs
We'd catch and release them
Through bushes
Pushing away spider webs
Stop - stop - listen -
See the slithering garden snake
And with daring precision
Lightening quick, grab below the head
Hold trophy high
- A victorious gladiator

The constant buzz of pesky mosquitoes
Swarming unkindly, attack arm and neck
With an angry slap - squash with a tinge of red
The bees buzzing, facet-eyed, spying blooms
Colorful butterflies bobbing, germinating flowers
From pistil to pistil, sucking sweet nectar
We'd catch the helpless winged specimens
Capture in a clouded glass jar
One more trophy, not thinking that life is sacred.

But that was yesterday or yesteryear
Anxious reflection I still hold dear?

LEAVING FOOTPRINTS

When we write we reveal
When we proclaim "yes" or "no"
When we pray in awe, we kneel
Our values and prejudices show

We are a reflection
Of our upbringing, of our birth
We are that human imperfection
That over/under values what we are worth

When someday we total our deeds on earth
When love, family, work save the treasure
Underline the reason for our birth
It's a big bill, too late to recoup its measure

So in a ghostly form we come and go
Some that we cared for, better we don't know
So with energy, enthusiasm, show respect
It's time to take a breather, dwell with nature and recollect

Imagine, stand so natural naked pure
Our temporary voyage here on earth to take a cure
All of us special, gifted in a thousand ways
Build on our knowledge and perception phase by phase

What reason, what mission
Rejuvenation, children revision
Like ants on earth's crust
We do it 'cause we must

Yet in mind a rumbling noise
Get hold, get hold
We do have choice
It's time to end, our tent must fold.

Imagination is boundless; nurture it while you still can

Frog Hopper, Reno Crafts Fair

FLASHES OF CHILDHOOD PART II

Lengthwise, roll down the hill
Tease, push, and wrestle
Pinch each other, as little boys do
Or catching the brown, beetle-like May bugs
Antlers on their male counterparts
Trap in spacious cigar box
Fill with green leaves
Abundant meal for the innocent insect

The rustle of windblown leaves
Brown, yellow, mountains
Half decomposed in the sun's rays
Dancing oblivious
Watching the sunbeam dance to
The cantata of chirping birds
Answering the mating call
With innocent chirps
Painting the landscape with
Nature's music.

Stepping between cow dung
Cows chewing, clinking cowbells
While the morning crow of the rooster
Announcing the dawn
Soothes the hens, jostles
Pink pigs in their messy pigsty.

Competitive, jumped from the roof of the barn shed
Into hay bales spread
Like a yellow mattress, oozing their fresh cut smell
Dry grass for the winter store
Jumped again - my right hand twisted
Fractured in two places
Utterly painful, my tears and anguish
Mixed with pride

The surprise of sudden rain
Often ignoring shelter
Soaked to the skin
All wet and natural
This time of bliss and innocence
The laughter of those moments
Embellished in my being
How lucky to remember once more
Reflect - 75 years later
With barely a scratch

I must have loved the world
As even today I can fly and fall,
Lift my bent, older, body erect
Smile content, excited with living
Not yet ready to define my memories
But ready for tomorrow
Tired eyes, refreshed

I wish you love and best of health
Still friends and self-contentment
Is your greatest wealth

Teenagers facing the adjustment to parents and family during adolescence.

There is definitely a change in your relationship as you develop physically and mentally through your teens.

Since you are dependent yet seeking your own independence, stress, anger and frustration may easily result. As a teenager you are trying to be mature yet are young simultaneously. You may have feelings of resentment towards your parents telling you what to do and laying down new rules, but you can't yet leave home.

There may be curfews of when to get home at night, and other restrictions. Often parents do not adjust to their teenagers' new identities. Often the way you dress and groom yourself is questioned and the way you act towards others. Often teenagers crave the latest type of music, lingo, dress and attitudes. Parents don't always understand these needs.

Parents' expectations may appear unreasonable at times. Usually, however, there is a good reason for their demands. But what choice do you, the teenager have?

As girls turn into more mature adults parents are worried about eating habits, pregnancy, boyfriends, peer pressure.

Life is a time to test, experiment and question, as you are in a growing stage. It is a time to "fit in", be accepted and be better understood. But these have to be done with caution and common sense, to avoid the dangerous pitfalls into which some teens fall.

Sometimes you may feel "out of it", or lack full self-confidence. The fact is, even as adults, all of us have periods where we are unsure, scared and feel self-conscious. It's OK sometimes to be a "loner", to say no, to withdraw a little, ponder, yet continue being a positive, active person.

> *Often you are unsure of what you are expected or want to do. "Is it wrong?", "Will I get caught?" The best advice is; when others are doing something dangerous, immoral, destructive or illegal you simply do not want to follow. Make up your own mind and do not be pressured.*

You also may now see your parents and family in a different light, for parents go through changes too as their children become teenagers.

I WOULD JUDGE

Addicted to late night TV
I binge to escape the real me
Absorbed in the visual inane
I would judge this person quite insane

*Competition brings out the best in us
But sometimes the most envious worst*

Blackhawk Automotive Museum, Blackhawk, CA

YOU ARE NOT GOD

After a long rest
Giant man is free
Chain untied
World ready, right
There is a storm about to brew
Man's joy of life, of love
Now rejuvenated new
About to consume and succeed
Unfathomable strength, impossible feat
Creative genius nurtured with amazing zest
The world so infinite, beautiful yet grotesque
In arrogance I want to rectify
Or put my earthen stamps
Move the mountain
Change the world

Huge colossus, your turn to shoot
Victory now or abort
Yet one bit of advice
I'll say it thrice

You are not God
You are not God
You are not God

HALF ASLEEP

If you awake at twilight time
Half rested, groggy, half sublime
Dared in the netherworld
A grey, uncertain curtain now unfurled

Where am I to go?
What to do?   I do not know
Should I recline, eyes closed refrain
Say goodbye   off to sleep again?

Half-baked, with great effort awake
Dare take the world on for the moment's sake
Laugh, cry or numbly observe
Until I strike my every titillating nerve

'Twas now, 'twas here, 'tis ever present still
Awake I choose my path and tame my will
Share joy, infect the air with love
Active, a doer all around blessed from above

The cycle of our day does end
We do adore, thankful as friend to friend
Observe the baby's cry to cheerlful giggling belly laugh
That babe was you or I, touched by the magic staff

To grow and live
To take shape and give
Back to rest and sleep
For what our mind has trapped
Captured and retain to keep

Sleep now, to rejuvenate, repair and heal
In full command to act upon what I now feel
Watch out, my desire now more certain
On center stage fulfill my act before a final drawn curtain

It's OK to reach high, but don't strain yourself!

MEDITATIVE THOUGHT

No matter how poor or rich
Tonight before eyes close
Escape your niche
Meditate. Reflect. Pray
With dignity. Inquire, self-respect

In a corner of your room
Where peace, compassion now does loom
Silently eyes open or close
Relax, breathe heavy out of mouth and nose
In contrast to the litany of hectic day
The power of the spirit now holds sway

Imagine jewels, rings, coins your life's treasure
Gone, nothing to lose
Material wealth replaced not choose
Prophetic inspiration of your "id"
This moment is yours to make your bid
You left an aching soul
Reborn in nature, feel so whole
No interdiction, no restriction

Dream-like peruse salve for your pains
Contracted angels upheld in chains
Unfurled nourished sustained, new venues now unfurled
Confusing aspects of our more macabre world
Tired, utter fatigue, I now retreat almost asleep
Timeout, at ease, a covenant to keep

Which virtue won
Which temptations now undone?
I close my eyes, I yawn
Weaker, tired, feel like a pawn
One aspect: sleep ignore
The other: face the spirit to the core
Were food, the clothes soon to disappear
Stripped of my outer garments,
I am what I am still here

I DO WHAT I CAN

He said
I am
I do what I can
I cannot change the sky and sea
They are so open, blue and free

Exuberantly I play
Run, exercise without delay
Share passions, friendships and sometimes pain
Knowing after sun may come the rain

> I am
> I do the best I can

If I get angry I'll explode
I'll let it out not get my goat
I'll stay calm and keep my cool
Better than being called a fool

> I am
> I'll do the best I can

So when I feel passionate about you
My hormones, testosterone ring so true
For you are close you are my friend
You share and let our feelings blend

> I am
> I'll do the best I can

Thanksgiving every day
In every way
In heart and mind is here to stay
Taste freedom, love, work and pain
Adventure of our life we do sustain

LET THE WORLD IN

Open the window, let the world in
Share   inhale
See the moon light beams
Craters, shadows in your eyes

Hear rustling leaves, walls of grey
Out in space things are not always what they seem
New sounds   smells without delay
Watch dust dance on an unlit beam

Cold air, warm air fresh and awake
Hustle   bustle
Gather your things, your soul
Leave, get out doors for goodness sake

With joy I share my inner heart
My longing feelings will not part
With you, for hand in hand
Confront nature's stirring element

What if it rains or snow comes inside?
What if grey dust permeates the air?
Just close the window
Let the world bounce off the window pane

With your heart pumping
Your mind ticking
There is an explosive creativity
In you
Go let it out!

WRINGING OUT THE MIND

when we wring out the mind

        always another
drop   of wisdom

slowdown

                                  patience

be honest

                                with thyself

        the orange
    FULLY squeeeezed

                The towel stopped
            d
             r
              i
               p
                p
               i
                n
                 g

the mind says
make this a healthy delicious me

the mind says

                    help!

really means it

                deny the mind

follow the mind

CONTROL

In youth we play with lives
We learn, experiment and thrive
Manipulate, cajole, threaten, place guilt
Punish and reward until our ego is filled

It starts with parents and their kids,
Intelligent and brawny pushing in our midst,
"Do this, do that" - a tenuous, scary cry
The receiver awed only he knows why

Once educated by life, deed and school
Ingrained controlling values now use this tool
Do this, do that - the lackey servant paid
Silently or quite direct we obey, unafraid

As we dominate and conjugate into old age
We mellow, still dictate the innocent old sage
The tide does turn and twist
Infirm and weak, still served our wishes now dismissed

You too are on the pecking order
Your turn long gone just look around the border
Go mellow, with sensitivity treat your companion with compassion
For you may be manipulated and treated in same fashion

So if the order is "do this, do that"
Thrill twice, before you reject with spat
It's called maturity and growing up
For you'll do what's right and simply stop.

No choice in our beginning
Not anxious for the end
Let's laugh and celebrate by singing
And question that which
Neither of us understands

Each time we walk by
The same place
The time and mood
Is different

LEARNERS

Some of us learn
Faster than others
Some learners erase their knowledge
With a closed mind
And wonder as they go
Why they never reach their goal

To be punctual and prompt
is a great step towards responsibility and success

Grandaughter Madison and Firefighter at the fair

ASPIRE

If you aspire,
But don't tire,
My envy, jealousy, and ire
From those who dream
But do not seem
Until they act,
To be exact.

The maker, doer,
Open, more honest, truer,
Is proud of all the polished or unpolished
Products that shine,
For all to witness, criticize each line.
Once done, the act, more need,
The value is in the doing and the deed.

Regroup, you cannot please every fan,
And start anew
To create again.

KING ON THE MOUNTAIN

Success begets success
Until on peak and mountaintop
An unexpected wind
Brings unpredictable weather
And I come down
Knowing I must bend to the elements
Even the king on the mountain
Soon leaves the pinnacle
Grateful to kiss the earth below

Life! Deeds we do and undo
We do live and learn yet learn not
The joy in giving is the gift

INNOCENCE OF YOUTH

Alert, enthralled jump into action
Young person meets the challenge great
Like a festive meal piled on the world, that is your fate
Mesmerized   pure   sheer   strong will
Conquer wrong, dissatisfaction grinding in the value mill

I choose, I choose
Youngster certainly surmises
New manipulation twists
Most shocking, bottom line surprises

The whales, the frogs, the trees
The poison seeping deep beyond our knees
Grain-fed ducks, precious fur from mink and fox
Carcinogens pollute earth water, a most killing pox

Then there are man's arrogant, stupid wars
There's cancer, heart disease, as HIV infections soar
Man combatant of man, man steals from man
Abhorrent, millions incarcerated in the can

Oh young one, your wingspan soaring with delight
World's landscape to be tilled so wide
Nourish, till and sweat at harvest time
Harvest of healing, of compassion in this rhyme

Revolt, redraw what is really true
Change nature, man into a golden glue
Of fairness, justice through new vision to survive
Harness the hate, religious strife, new vision to new life

Oh you blue, black, brown green-eyed hope
So young and innocent blood boiling
With man's other, optimum world elope
Discard the weeds, spread the seeds

A SPIT IN THE OCEAN

Life is a pittance
A spit in the ocean,
Precious as a fine cut diamond,
A rock tossed into the ocean,
Lost among sparkling brown pebbles and myriads of sand stones
That erect creature of destiny, the Sphinx
Questions our hunger to touch the very stars glistening in the sky
And she wonders at our immense appetite
As we consume flora and fauna, drink from virgin wells
Leave abundant waste, decay and chemicals
Watch pure, clear liquid become rivers of poison
And she, gigantic and beautiful wonders
That we justify our existence
By forever procreating, building awesome nests
That we dig deep into the breast of the earth
Transform lush nature
Into cold and shining cities
Create myriads of beehive inventions
Are born into a world of genetics and new specimens
Thrust and pushed into fashionable particularity
Rocket to Mars, the moon and the stars
Create mutants and replicas,
She sees us engulfed and drowned in our own humanity
Gasping for air in the sea of the universe

We fish and fish the oceans far
Fish species disappear
In place synthetic food's our star
They even have synthetic beer

In the long run honesty goes far
But a white lie bridges the moment
Until your conscience drives you nuts

They say we're modern,
yet we still use toilet paper.

Before the Storm

The rippled placid water
Becalmed icy melt
At sequoia tree trunk
Absolute silence
Isolate at midnight
Away from civilization
A slow, relaxed, beating
Heart content
Snowshoes at 11,000 feet
All these spell tranquility earned
A fleeting, lucky time
Before the next snowstorm

A blank page need not always be filled
to bring out the thought and meaning...

Alien Invasion

DARE ME

I, the seed of seeds from Adam or before
I alive, searching this great earth
    that I adore
I, a microcosm, grain amongst mankind living
Eager to meld, wide joy of giving

Dare me, care for me, spare me
Touch my life
Stir the juices, shapes
    that I thrive
Now here is my moment, my time
Echo, mold and shape, I'm in my prime

The single chain of deeds that feeds
Work, fun and grieving all are meshed
Autumn harvest gathers, shaken, thrashed
Here's to the fruit, the loot to suit

Stray not, disappoint me not, your seed now grieving
Put me on your pedestal, forever feeling
    Great in need distrust, but still believing

Growing, growing, maturing
Inert - feel the great grandeurs of life

I wonder what tomorrow brings?

RAIN

It's 12:37 A.M.
Gusts, sheets of torrential rain
Incessant   loud   thrashing wet
Continuous, heavy drumming sound
Proud   most defying
Never dying

Everywhere, pools of soggy wet
The rows of silvery pearls bounce on their target
Receptive leaves deliver the cool liquid
Like teaspoon medicine gone wrong
Drip-drop unto the ground
A distant thunder (barely audible) pronounced eerie
Evidence of more to come.
Roof drains rasping, moving into lower level places
Spilling the translucent moving liquid
The rivulets into roaring dirty, erratic waves
A torrent monster, unstoppable
Umbrella, roof, cover!
Nature's foreboding warning, a buzzing noise
Soon ebb and flow diminish
Rain-flood, so omnipotent has its own life
Sending a message
We huddle, under cover, trying to listen to music or TV
We are aware of nature's brunt
We are dry! We are safe - for now

Then   drip   drip   ping.
The gutter rattles, the window pane repels
Is it ever over?

Can you not feel it as it wets your cheek?
The downpour rushes into the creek
The sneakers soaked - moist - wet
Mother nature once again won the bet

PRICE TAG

Some critics, clowns so perfect
Some so vain
With quick tongue shower mockery
They think they entertain

At school I, mostly well dressed
Forgot to remove my price tag
To that I will attest
It was an oversight - so rest!

        The snob in back of me pointed out the tag
        In front of the others; chided, the snobby nag
        And she's hardly the type to brag

        Yes, she did ridicule
        I was embarrassed and just not cool
        For a moment mocking, she did rule
        Yet she really teased and I'm the fool

        I, the recipient ask: "Was
this demeaning act so really cool?
Or was the buffoon the silly fool?
It's easy to make fun of others
To mock and ridicule
Much easier than looking in one's mirror
And hear the angels wail and drool".

He who laughs first
Has a head start
and can chuckle ever after

I'd rather be right
But if I erred,
I'd only be human

TOPPLE THE KING

At the pinnacle of control
Bring 'em down! The new confrontational goal!
Bring me down and I'll kill!
Let's knock that king off the hill!

Our competitive nature says go, be a getter
Surpass competition, exert to be better
Using clever knowledge devious means to surpass
Goal to succeed, to be first in the class

Yet we dare trample over ruins to reach the top
Competitors at the way side, ignored and don't stop
Defeated, enemies are left behind
Our balanced, jovial personality now crass, so unkind

Call it success, winning the part
Lonely on top, the battle won hard
In this aspiring contest full of guts and nerve
Can we retain human conscience, get what we deserve?

Can we still be grateful, a bit humble?
Or rough wielding giants lost in a jungle
Can we balance, re-appraise
A touch of human kindness and grace

Foolish victors thinking they can win every race
Of course not! Restore a touch of compassion and grace
Maybe see the blessing in humankind
Open eyes and heart show we're not so blind

Do we have to lose a bit of our soul
To heal, make ourselves whole?
Hope, coupled with determination pays
We dare return to society with new, mature and wiser face

Brilliant, successful people can also do the most stupid things...

WE MARCH

Mostly we slither, walk or crawl
Cajole, rejoice, blatantly brawl
This time we march
In unison
Though not in step

We march
For justice, fairness
For moderation, not excess (unless)
For nature's preservation
Self-destructive, the planet's population
We march for babies loved and cared
For old, crippled pain diminished and spared
For science and research
Disease, sicknesses we must purge

We march
For hope, for fairness of fellow man
Fortuitous share our lifetime span
For less desire in material things
For feelings equal to the leaders and kings
For less vanity
For less insanity

We march
For the arts
The painter, poet, writer
Musician, singer, soul-enlightener
For the of show of athletes great
We hail the icons, shout their fate
Icons with money, riches
Dazzle us, performance stars
For them, with them
We march

Olympic Torch Celebration, Ferry Building, San Fransisco, CA

We march
Most of all for will and cause
Our belief balances, better loves
Lucky in a sea of freedom's air
We can express, partake and dare
We are tiny ants on mankind's giant globe
The actors, protagonists of hope

We march
As symbols, flags of voice
We march to change society, provide some choice
We march to right some wrong
We know the world so small
Can be so much better

We march
together
into the unending horizon

*It's my turn, I thought, until I was pushed aside
and learned the facts of life*

51

VICTORY IN DEFEAT

He, who in defeat can muster, stands most erect
For him or her I bow with deep respect
He who dares with vengeance to get even in contempt
The challenge is to stay away from such anger pent
You loser, you hater, there's a life of challenge far ahead
Keep your venom far away from me, a pricey toll
Clear out your head, regroup the mind and muscle now instead
It's good to lose at times, appreciate the whole
It's healing love that nourishes my soul

You know the miserable loser never did appear
Saber's sharp for battle, that's why I am now here

Sometimes it's hard to acknowledge our world
It's here, it's all you have, in front of you a pearl
Green fields, deep valleys so admiring
Lost in the canyon streets so awe inspiring
Return in spirit, see your zest of youth
Break nasty habits away from home and narrow booth

It's the participation, give it all your best
So if you win or lose you did it as an earthly guest
The fun and joy advent of new game you will master
Go play participate, the dice rolling ever faster

And now fulfilled you feel so good
You did your best, you understood
For all the love and challenge 'tis just a game
Victorian struggle won, you'll never be the same

Those who criticize the most
Often are their own most
Deadly self-critics
And tortuously have to
Put up with themselves.

I am grateful for most things I have, and I'm not talking about money or possessions

CLOSENESS

Sometimes we seek the
voice of a friend
Other times the mind meets
the body, the touch
Break bread and value warmth
In the temporary bliss

The sparks of the mind
listen and share
Close - we snack and sip the nectar so divine
heal wounds of disagreement most benign
Absorb, enrapture in self-adulation
However confined in
mutual adoration
Let's hug, smile with glee
my locker or yours
close - embrace alive
hearts beat

Exult in heaven's passion play
contain the vibes
the feelings stay
enmeshed, two of a tribe

The voice, the look, magic encounter
the momentary trance of bliss
the hormones dancing now in each
true body language and with a kiss

Feel the energy, the warmth
closeness of voice, magician's wand
the hidden love
two merged into
one

BUZZBOMB

(I wrote this in June of 1945 when 50,000 American prisoners of war were suddenly freed with the German collapse and flown to an obscure tent city for 20,000 called Lucky Strike (after the cigarette), near Rouen, France. I was shipped there from Liege, our combat Engineer Base, as a temporary clerk helper for three weeks. Then recalled to my unit, which was ready to fight the Japanese who still engaged us in WWII. Buzzbomb was a real fuzzy mutt, a terrier.)

"Buzz-Bomb," I yelled. Soon before me stood the little creature with its wiggling long tail, and those gleaming eyes. Buzz-Bomb was the cute little brown pup we had picked up during the early stages of the V-I and V-II raids on London. While we were in the Midlands near Shrewsbury building Baily bridges and in the heart of London, during the Buzz bomb raids, the dog had grown up, the pride of the company. He had gone with us during training; lived and slept in out tents, ate our chow, and only differed from a soldier in that he never barked back.

By the time we crossed the channel on the LST, Buzz-Bomb was considered a traveling dog. Buzz-Bomb had two exceptional qualities, one being that he would run away, but always return. The other occurred at night. He was watchful and would loudly bark at strangers coming nearby. It was during those wet, stalling days in December, near the German border that Buzz-Bomb made a name for himself.

We had just arrived and our company split into three platoons. Our position was near a deserted shot-up village. Since there was not much activity, we only had two guards out, the front being several miles away. The time was just before the Battle of the Bulge when the Wermacht, exerted to the last effort, started the counter offensive.

The author and Buzzbomb the dog during WWII, France, 1945

German patrols and fifth-columnists, aided by paratroopers, infiltrated into our lines, caught many units off guard, and at the time captured many men, including valuable booty. We were weary from the day's fatigue, and with the exception of the guards, everyone was fast asleep. All of a sudden, in the pitch darkness, there was a sudden loud bark. We all awoke and by natural instinct reached for our guns, while some of us held our pistols ready. Under orders from the lieutenant, we quietly slipped away. It was useless to fight a foe that we could not see. One of our guards was missing and the action seemed to be much closer.

No sooner had we taken the first step back that the dog began to bark, warning us. We must have been only a hundred yards away. Than a loud BANG! A yelp. They had shot the dog. We knew now where their location was. We reached our unit, informed the C.O. and soon came orders for a temporary retreat. We had been saved from whatever the Jerries had planned for us by the poor dog. Never shall I forget the warning bark of Buzz-Bomb, who for once never returned.

Sometimes in life no-one wins,
and we can walk away in peace

Yad Vashem, Israel Holocaust Martyrs' and Heroes' Memorial

AN ODE TO MY PEN

Between my index finger and thumb
A precious pen immobile dumb
Until, directed by my brain,
This gifted instrument at dance again
In spirited circles and gyrations
Pens mark inordinate sensations.

"I love you, miss you" now in tune
The rhapsody of love begins to swoon
Or bitter words, "I'm so ashamed"
All the while I know I'm framed!
On paper soon the soul pours out
A litany of feelings from the fountain spout.

And oh, once written, kind and unkind drivel so embossed
The receptor ready in all anger, challenge tossed
The written accusations in red dripping ink
A warning for the bare-knuckled bout in bloody rink.
Once on the computer carefully announced
The critic's hammer proudly pounced.

Ah, so much do I like and love my pen
Again, again and then again I am the greatest fan
With this great tool I pour out my fondest wish
Or drool; send out a recipe of favorite dish
Too many bills, in debt up to my neck
Pen will soon help me write and pay that check.

It was the pen that crafted our constitution
Or freedom's manifesto that proclaimed the revolution
Or Homer, Plato, Aristotle with the stroke of pen
Their wisdom mark made us their eternal fan
Or when Karl Marx or Engel, with pen proclaimed
Communist manifesto in which the workers framed.

Or chronicles from kingdom's past
The history of most promiscuous cast
Or Vatican libraries explode with pen's art
For pen, word and mind are never far apart.
I reiterate, I simply love my pen and it's strength,
My deepest feelings written at great length.

Ecstatic I communicate,
I sign the documents, I even sign my fate
The words like thrashing waves express
My past, my now, my wishes to possess.

Each pen at master's bidding so profound
Sincere and honest scribbling do abound
Sometimes a smudge shows writer's tears
Most often greetings from close dears
And sometimes writings are so grotesque
Embarrassed to meet the tests and requests.

And oh, when Kugelschreiber suddenly turns blank
Another pen replaces at first rank
The execution now on paper does proclaim
Washington, Jefferson and Lincoln's name
Or writer's autograph, one from a movie star
The egotist will share his writings wide and far.

Oh yes, I love my pen
Can hardly wait again
To sit at valley's riverside
Compose the lovely sonnets for my bride
Or in autobiography describe my life in great hilarity
With pen a touch left to posterity.

No matter which mood I'm in the pen is at my bidding
It will record vast compliments or naughty at each sitting
Or if downhearted and slightly depressed
With pen explore and heal as I confess
The power of the pen indeed
To change the world, a revolutionary seed.

JUST HAPPINESS

If I were a woman instead of a man,
Or a woman who could and still can
Be ambidextrous, bi, or confused,
If two spirits in one could be fused,
What would the critics write to be amused?

But I am ME!
Solid, energetic, free!
Maybe rattled, rated, berated,
Shaking off showers of advice,
All I want is to feel, to love, to be nice.

Earn my being, my wage,
No wise man or sage,
No muse, no witch, no queen,
No king, don't care if I'm private or out to be seen.

All I want is to follow my avocation,
Laugh, have fun, be amused without ration
To share the world's burden, help the poor
Pray, work and make peace not war

We are all touched by goodness and hex,
We know our sex is most complex,
We breathe and we think; we are not blind,
Just simple happiness we want to find,

AND KEEP!

Boisterous and noisy teens are in their element
As all of us were in our time
Reek of innocence

It's easy to boast and brag
To cajole and nag
Much harder to dream
Work your way up to the cream
Say, it's real hard; I learned it
Thank you, but I also earned it

> *What seems like chaos*
> *Could be constructive breakdown,*
> *Ready to be rebuilt*

Some of us don't like to look back
But the past is really also in front of us,
And has been with us all the time

> *Dogged perserverence down the wrong track*
> *May land you up against the wall*
> *Or flat under the wheel*

Wisdom tempered by caution
Can be your stepping stone to self contentment

> *The road of good intentions*
> *can be paved with gold, kindness, perserverence*
> *and hot air*

You can have the last laugh
As long as it's not on me

> *All must have its end*
> *Even though you may have missed*
> *the beginning*

Careful you don't outsmart yourself!

> *Our bodies are made up of mostly water and bones*
> *So we may just float away*

Notes from the Poet

LISTEN! LISTEN!

"Listen, listen," I smartly told my grandson B, now nineteen.

"Why listen to that old goat?" he probably said to himself. He might even have tuned me out. Here, at eighty-five years (times 365 days!), still with a keen mind, I say, "hear me!"

Yes, I survived my teens. I was dreamer - mostly concerned only with next day or next week. I had that first crush, the usual dreams about this beautiful chick. I spent restless nights before an important test or ball game. I was often angry - too many bosses! Everyone was telling me what do. Yes, mostly I did as I was told, though sometimes regretfully. Inside of me was a person in my own right and I wanted some recognition. And I wanted good grades.

As a youth, I lived like a half orphan with different families, sponsored by some social organization or another, and often felt pangs of loneliness. Much around me was unfair.

Yes, I was lucky enough to gulp down a good hamburger once in a while, yet never was invited to parties. Had no guidance. Just dreams. Today, eight-five years later I have knowledge, experience, feelings, thoughts and those are everything.

While you are just starting your life, I probably should be counting my days. But I don't want to. Too much to do. Too much to love, too many good ball games, theater, shows to see. Too many places to visit, too many girls (or just one!) to kiss. It's still all ahead of me. You have seventy years to catch up with me!

CARE FOR THE BRAIN

How to fill my brain
Thought sustain
First by experience to store
Education much galore
Memorize and synthesize
Experiment and realize
Eat right food
Message, get in right mood.
Use it - don't abuse it.
Care - then again,
You have one brain
One precious brain
To guide you
For LIFE

**the word
SANE
with prefix
IN
is questionnable
but easy to prove**

CASHMERE SWEATER

I thank the beast
Whose hair I wear and feast
It's hugging, covering my upper frame
I understand the sheep so shorn
Will again be the same
Once new growth of hair
Its nakedness repair

Alpaca wool, cashmere
Plain or fancy design knit
When it's chilly cold
I hold this sweater dear
Wear walking or where I sit

So thank you shearer, knitter
As this gorgeous sweater
In all the comfort
I feel fitter
Aren't the little things refined?
So pleasant to the body and the mind?

CHALLENGE ADVERSITY

Each beam on us glistens
With heaven's protection
Yet it is up to us to do,
To plant, choose in each election
The juice of nature's drink
As we challenge our adversity
In a fighting stance and fighting ring
Prove worthy with delight
For nature's victorious honor
Gives hope and
Makes things right
Easy you say?
No, it takes strain and guts

**Another war?
When will our egos shrink?
(they call it national security)**

Is your life like a circular staircase?
An escalator or the waves of an ocean?
Or maybe a delicious feast
Or confused upside down
Don't worry gravity and time straighten you out.

STORIES

Sailing, sailing 48,000 feet
550 miles an hour
120 sardine-packed passengers
Somewhere beyond the Mississippi
Over the clouds
The white marshmallow clouds
While sunlight glistens
10 million stories down below

Which one is yours?

AGE AND YOUTH

In youth, for youth, for you,
Age has endless boundaries.
Learning, seeking,
energy, enthusiasm, a blind eagerness
Whereas the older generation,
Experienced, tamed by time and nature,
Slowed by man and life
Still has the thrust and sight of unparalleled, unlimited vision
With life an ever-changing kaleidoscope.

"The difference?" you asked,
between unspent youth and limited age
Is in the morrow, what we do and think,
With or without life's extended consequences and rewards.

Yet we all face THE NOW.
Our heart is beating, our mind alive,
Rich and rife.
It's the perception and the willingness to act swiftly
that makes the old more cautious.

Still, is the doer, the doer,
regardless of the chasm of division of generations?
Hours are precious, short.
The minutes steal away, never to return.
Each generation must measure, treasure deed and time
In their own mysterious way.

If you have to cry, wait until I give you a better reason

Mother said, "You must clean your plate"
That's where all my troubles began

ECSTATIC ENERGY

Kill time outdoors
Pure light blue sky tinged with white
Announces Spring - this warming bright day
Excites the mind
Nerves titillating
Feeling the rebirth
Of Freshmen and romance

Testosterone under the skin explode
Sizzling to jump out of your skin
The mind bombarded sparks
Ringing the bells of bright visions
Hormones too tumultuous
The afternoon sun bears heroically
On this special day of firsts

All I wanted was a book from the library
But I got a sunful of happy beams
To last me through the afternoon
You may call it a waste of time
To me, it was another celebration of the season
Sometimes the most simple is the best;
Time and nature do the rest

Empty Mind

The empty mind
Filling like a glass of water
Invisible, weighty liquid
Refilling all the nerve endings
Like a computer
Reacts most powerfully
First chemical reaction
Stimulation
Then
All hell broke loose

*They say "You can do better!" and when you do,
they say "You can do better!"*

I FIDDLE MY DAY AWAY

Whilst raiding the fridge where I don't belong
Listen to a snappy, melodious new song
Email, watch TV, chat with friends and share
When I slow down I remind myself I care

I fiddle my day away

With baseball, football, basketball or other
Walk to the store, hang with friends or my brother
Take the bus, a plane, a train
Deliver goods and home again

Text my folks and then my friends
It's time to quit for the night and make amends
Try to work and be good at school
Nature, machines, laptop is my tool

I fiddle my time away

I'm not a judge or president or chief
I fill my hours quickly, set in my belief
Be a scholar, artist or great at sports
Stay out of trouble and out of courts

We all fiddle our lives away

*Sing me a song of healing and solace
And I sing one of hope
Torn out of my inner soul*

*I put the chocolate away
but it teased my imagination and I ate it anyhow*

EGO TO FEED

Challenge - a bright spot
Dare study a lot
Goal to succeed
Ego to feed

Some like twitter
Non-doers sitter
Easily give up
There's the rap

If you have a talent and a will
Seek independence, pay us your bill
Willing to learn
The more you'll earn

Long road ahead
Hard work instead
Sometimes long tedious hours
Use all your persuasive powers

You simply can't stop
You mustn't give up
So much good ahead
Easier to be well-read

Often not fair
Yet we care
Trust family, friends
Heal, make amends

*CalShakes dog sculptures,
Shakespeare Theater, Orinda, CA*

*Some things are better not understood
unless you want to grow up too fast*

Notes from the Poet

CAN I SHARE THIS WITH YOU?

Sure, a great baseball glove, a tennis racket, an iPhone, a bike, a computer: they all are a must.

Maybe some pocket change if you are in need. Not ready yet to run away? No matter how grim, there's no place like home where you probably have some of these material wants. Maybe you are lucky and even have your own room. I have a whole two story house just for me; I earned it! So ask yourself from time to time, "What do I want in life?" or "Who am I really? Where is my place and where am I going with school, friends, family? What are my goals?"

Every new day is a surprise. Headlines scream about war, murder, honors, and prominent politicians. You may be too busy just getting by, your favorite music, TV, friends, texting, Facebooking. But think, "Yes, I am me, and I am still growing. I have room to adjust."

Ha, you are indeed still growing - in body and brains and knowledge and experience. Imagine, too, I'm eighty-five and I still learn all the time! I see my grandkids busy with soccer, baseball, Scouts, music and such. You are all smart and yet wet behind your ears. So much to learn!

In short, all the fun, the dreams, the pain you have, remember that others around the world have them too. Life deals you all kinds of hands, and often the cards are stacked against you. So reshuffle and play another day.

So, since you are smart, I want to share bits of my wisdom. Here is a bit of free advice:
Read bits at a time. Think about them. Shape them to your needs. People can tell you what to do, but only you decide what you want to do, what is the right thing to do. Life is an equalizer - we all have to put up with some pressure and criticism, even the President of the United States! How you deal with it is the key.

Did you bring your Mom (or wife or girlfriend) flowers this year? Did you ever say or write "thank you" sincerely? Have you gone out of your way and helped anyone this week?

Remember: if you can make things better for yourself, it's your joy to feel. YOU CAN AND WILL ALWAYS IMPROVE YOURSELF. It's in the learning, making mistakes, getting a bit burned that teaches you when to step back, when to compromise, when to give in, even if you believe you are dead right! Pick your battles. Sure, always stick to your best principles. Hopefully you have been taught honesty, hard work, charity, how to say "thank you" and how to be grateful.

Just you live to be eighty-five, and you too can spout off!
"Why do you write this stuff at eight-five?" you ask. Because I love mankind. I really do. I know you may suffer. I know you will feel guilt. I know you will fail at times or stumble. So what? All great and small people have their shortcomings, why should you be any better? None of us is perfect.

IN MY OWN BACKYARD

Help
Us
That
Our garden
May prosper
In peace

IT'S NEVER TOO LATE

Huff and puff won't do it.
When something doesn't work,
Try something else,
Evaluate
take risks,
Get out of the usual,
What to do next -
Have some assurance of success
It's never
too late

Can you meet the challenge?

BURY THE HATCHET

The feat, to get up and not be angry
Get even - rage/revenge?
No - no, bury the hatchet;
"They can't do that to me - so unfair

I'll get him back soon enough"
The seed of getting even grows
Affects the mind
The impulse of utter helplessness

I must figure a way to vent my anger
So what? So what?
There'll be other friends
Betrayal, lies exist from earliest times

Think of the positive, the good
Before the negative diggers bury you
"You are worthy - the heck with them!"
So much to do - call, text, visit

Movie, get something to eat
Talk to family or another friend
It is a fun but sometimes disappointing world
In which we cope and stay cool

*Charity and forgiveness may heal your soul
but the pain lingers on...*

*The bragger soon stumbles over his own verbosity
and has his mouth stuffed*

MENTAL TEEN DANCE

Frigid, frightened, he skirted
Away from she who flirted
And like an octopus embraced
Him, spinning his equilibrium laced

What once was a strong position
Now is awkward, much indecision
Like frightened mouse or grouse
He'd rather hide in corner of his house

But closeness, chemistry of amour
A twosome dance a bit unsure
They hugged, they kissed
A certain distance she'd insist

For minutes together as one
Close, most electric feeling has begun
Into the hurricane called romance
Yet reticence not ready to make a change

So our young-loved minds bedazzled
Next day their vision with love frazzled
It's courting, sorting time
Little does youth know how lucky in its prime

Enthusiastic Thank You

Civility
Self-control
It's easy to complain -
Much harder to say, "Sorry!"
(Compliments a plus, with enthusiasm)
A " Thank You" - that counts!
Gnawing anger to be dusted with forgiveness
Great is the person who is earnest and sincere!

Why not try it sometime?

Forget

Some are meticulous, never forget
You often beget, always regret
Then there are things you'd rather never get
Can't erase them out of your head
Until the brain is so fully loaded
Guilt, anxiety, almost exploded
Best ease the pain, take your time
You'll be fine
You see
Unless you're as forgetful as me

COMPETITIVE DRIVE

If no-one is perfect, why strive?
To outdo, beat, to be alive?
To show our human spirit, to exceed?
To feed on inner urging and need?

And yet is not clothing and food enough;
Do we have to compete and hang so tough?
Where is the happy means
The balance to satisfy it seems?

Is it the inner wish to outdo and excel
Nurtured by parents "Must do well!"
Or is this drive within our genes
Those devilish inner activists, those fiends

Give me a challenge, I'll be there
A good contest shows I care
For how else can I then be better
Ascend the rungs of the highest ladder?

For I am good, for I am ME
What I do and get is what you see
To educate and better myself each day
Watch my deed, watch what I say

And show my guts, my worth
Treasure every day here on earth
Show honest love to family and friends
Rejoice in blessed deed make sense

And thank myself for what I've done
It won't be easy, not always fun
I'll face the challenge and will not run
Relish the richness of the nourishing sun

For in this crazy world to be alive
My inner peace fuels my every drive
And if I win or lose it doesn't matter
For tomorrow I'll strive to do even better

> *Go back to sleep, it's the middle of the night*
> *Relax and count your sheep*
> *As somewhere at the other end of the earth*
> *they fight*

MR. GOOD AND MRS. MEAN

Mr. Good and Mrs. Mean
Decided to go to a party.
Compliments by Mr. Good
Snide remarks from Mrs. Mean
"You don't know anything," she exhorted
"Maybe I don't," Mr. Good said,
"But I sure enjoy helping people, caring and giving"
"Poppycock," rattled Mrs. Mean,
"Why help, they don't deserve it."
Soon a little girl came with auburn hair and ponytails
And a great big smile.
"Would you like some cookies?" she asked as she held
Up the plate graciously.
"Oh, thank you, yes," Mr. Good retorted.
"Go away little girl," Mrs. Mean said in an unfriendly
Manner and turned away.
And so they lived unhappily ever after.

WALK WITH GRACE

Distinct urge to write
Show you I'm on your side
All have setbacks in our life
We battle to overcome and the strife

But many good things happened in the past
Your learning, love, life a blast
You've been successful and victorious
So many shining joyous weeks so glorious

Some time there's gravity, bleak days ahead
Dealt cards of dismal pain instead
And all the wishes, prayers for naught
Disease within now festers, caught

But please be hopeful, strong, survive
For all of us have but one short life
Make each day count for what it is
A token joy and a laugh or bliss

Even in adversity there is a ray of sun
A new day devours the night just done
And if you treasure every little delight
Remember we are with you, by your side

From tunnel of restriction into light
Learn, read, plan do it right
It's OK if you slip, fall on your face
Simply get up and walk away with grace

Better to venture
Do it now
Than soon forget
And not know how

I feel more scared   than happy sometimes
When I receive   too much good news

WHO ARE WE REALLY?

Every day evolves, revolves
With gravity we experience
The momentary colossal happenings
So that the work of innocence
Ends in a feast of doing
Building, moving around
Mountains of food and materials
We, too busy, don't even think about it
We shovel earth into dams
Fill up land with streets and houses
Ever so big canyons of office towers
Cars, planes, buses humming
To the anvil into a crescendo that we call life
We are that automaton, always busy
So easily we love and hate
Forgive but not forget
We are the dreamers, schemers,
Live on our own isle
Pulled into the mainstream of doing
We touch many
And many touch us
And sometimes we even say

Thank you

Half determined, half scared
Should I? Shouldn't I?
The torrent of vascillation
"Do somthing already!"
I sat down, pondered, and did absolutely the opposite

REBIRTH

Creative juices now at an ebb
Relaxed replayed a pleasant rap
Did not have to stab or shoot
Optimum behavior not at all rude

Too late for our tomorrow
Touch of joy and happiness I will borrow
And if luck fails and all's not well
Most determined pass up hell

Too late the arms and legs have disappeared
Top of head by a fire seared
And all mankind has lost their speech
Tower of Babel out of reach

Ballet sculpture, Jerusalem, Israel

But with stamina and determination
We'll ascend to a higher station
Each grain of sand so precious in possession
Bury the corpse, rebirth in every session

Watch It Grow

If love suddenly lands in your lap
Cuddle it
Cater to it
Cajole it
Watch it grow

Each weekend morn
New spirit is reborn
Exhaust our inner pleasure
It's in the doing we find a treasure

WHAT MAKES ME TICK?

I do not know what makes me tick
Sometimes I pinch myself to know it's not a trick
I know from heart goes to the brain
And to all membranes back and forth again

I shudder at the awful thought
Now what has our true nature wrought?
Still, lucky to have our friends
Many happy, helping hands

Challenging disposition
Decisively make decision
But most my love begs in desire
I love you clear, I am on fire

GETTING AHEAD

Just when we think
We are getting ahead
We are behind instead
The target moves,
The goal has changed
Life therefore, recon-
structed
Newly re-arranged

PEACE

The greatest gift some bring
Not to entertain and sin
But through persuasion vie for peace
For harmony and brotherhood to please
Diminish strife and conflict avoid war
For mankind tired - war and more

But first hate and revenge cast aside
Enemy now like new bride
Contemptuous of killing devastation
Research the banner peace flies over our nation
So we are vigilant for harmony and peace
So that our children's key will open gate to please

So Noble prize cherish dear
Persuasive highway of peace is near
And we can learn to tolerate with great respect
To solve world's problems with our intellect
And learn to share in joy again
A peaceful future in the main

PROPRIETARY INFORMATION

one sock on
the other ripped
I put it on
no-one but me
can see the hole
and I will not tell

a single soul

*The difference between the poor and rich
Is that the rich have tax shelters
And the poor have tents*

CREATE A CLIMATE OF HAPPINESS

It is criminal to cheat yourself of fun
Treat each day as if your life has just begun
Start with a healthy meal,
Pinch yourself that you are real

So much to live for a rip-roaring rife
Exciting productive, you are so alive
Listen to cool new music, so upbeat
Percussion sounds beat so neat

Every joyful exercise
Give yourself first prize
Share your spirit with your love
Know there's protection from above

Only you can help, shape your day
Earned love and compliments will come your way
If things turn sour don't give up
Not easy to climb to the mountaintop

Read amusing magazines
Revert with energy as in your teens
Know that your best days are still ahead
Dream great dreams after an early bed

GENEROSITY

He wanted to STEAL my gal
But when he noticed the price tag
He changed his mind
In generosity he let me KEEP her

We all have bones to pick - Better make sure
Our own bones are in order

FUNKY PEOPLE

Foolish, frivolous, full of zest
Fortunately, figuratively speaking, few survive
Few meet the test
A little funkiness enriches, say
Makes us smile, out of the way
Too much, too much - furtive and frolic
Fervently we must escape the fragmented mile

*Most of us have a budget.
The trick is how far to stretch it.*

ADVICE FOR TEENAGERS

Listen, listen no extremes
Life's still good, not what it seems
Not everyone in school's so perfect
Do not join destructive gang or sect

                              Best to exercise and eat decent food
                              To keep you in a good and happy mood
                              Fewer soft drinks, avoid the booze
                              For teenagers always that's bad news

The world sometimes seems so sick
You shoot straight and right turn pick
It's OK to disagree
There are many angles to the things we see

                              Sometimes like a pup you bark and yelp
                              It's OK to openly ask for help
                              Like an arrow try to shoot straight
                              Sometimes patience; have to wait

Remember like all in teenage years
There's time for fun and time for tears
But millions on this earth all made it
You too can live through and take it

                              Best to read, and read a lot
                              To be informed that is the act
                              You can also Google, Yahoo and Bing
                              At fingertips find just about everything

Since on your elders you depend
Help out, listen and emend
'Tis not easy, I admit
You're not Einstein, just a growing kid

                              If you dare take drugs or dope
                              Eat your brains out; cannot cope
                              And if at times the cards aren't right
                              Self-control; avoid the fight

So eat lots of fruit and veggies too
Run and walk or join a crew
Discipline yourself although it's hard
Do all your homework and stay smart

                              Parties, dances are OK
                              No funny business while you play
                              Be polite, dare try your way
                              It's quite normal, have your say

CROWD

Get along with the in crowd
Hang out all about
Older leaders may do some stuff
Thye're never satisfied, not enough

It's OK - part of a benign gang
Bond, friends - do not harangue
Still, when it comes to drugs
Leave before the pressure bugs

We all want to be part
Of friends that hang from the very start
Sometimes, sometimes I am scared
To cross the line - I'm not prepared

So lucky to be with friends
Drink, eat, enjoy the merriments
And if the raucous party gets out of hand
You'd better leave before the end

FRIENDSHIP

The morrow most unknown
What we have, try to hold our own
And often lose, things disappear!
But friends and love are real
Beyond the anguish is true, is joy, we feel
So thank you master, somewhere out in space
To have invented friendship
In the magic of the human race

Do celebrate your success
It comes rarely, I confess
Better than failure on a platter
But when you're happy all this doesn't really matter

HOW HIGH IS HIGH?

How high is high?
How low is low?
Is it beyond the sky
Or molten below, far below?
Until you've been there,
You'll never know.

Deceive, perceive, believe
From mighty height
To earth, gravity levels all pride
Suddenly you swoop down
Grimace, distorted face, disjointed, frown
Why did you let me down?

Yet, from the depth of the nether world
A magic spiral staircase unfurled
Step upward into sun and light
Perceive injustice now on the steps of right.
Slay the dark dragon on the spot
Let his carcass reek and rot

Write, speak-up, raise your voice
Recover, stronger, adjust, head held with poise
To earth, forget the heaven and the hell,
It's now, it's here, I do, and act, and tell.
Gain recognition and respect
You simply have to act

There is always another message board on the computer -
Too many inundate and drown me
Help! I am coming up for air!

DOORS

Imagine yourself, your life
Which doors have you entered?
Ah, so many each and every day
Do you see the doors?

From space to space
In the privacy of our homes
The bathroom, basement and attic
Doors that hold secrets

You know you can enter or exit
Unsure of what you might find
Parents young, bidding
Full of love, endearing

Doors of many colors
Great hopes
Openings of fear, frustration
Doors I never want to enter again

Doors once opened
Part of my youth
(If you play with pet birds
Never leave the door open)

Doors are merely extensions of
Our boxed-in lives
Doors of separation, of sound
Of smell, of life

Truly doors are not natural
Where in the mountains and valleys
The expanse of open meadows
Do you see doors?

Once the spark in us is ignited
Watch out! We'll challenge the world!

LIESELOTTE 1941

Lieselotte snapped out of her slumber
The nine year old, petite, precocious girl,
Crammed next to Mutti in this stinking cattle car.
The cramped humanity, barely room to sit or lie,
Clothes for three days, no latrine
Old, sick, coughing, indigent
Several had died already as the wagons moved on.
Ever so often they would open up the rolling doors
Somewhere in the country.
Always the uniformed, angry guards
With their rifles, guns, dogs, harsh commands
They said, "On the way to the East; Poland!"
The sad, eerie sound of wailing, whining,
The endurance of pain - all but mesmerized
The clatter of the railroad wheels below ever moving.

It was barely fourteen months ago,
Their beautiful large apartment in Berlin
Oriental carpets, book cases with leather-bound books
Lots of oil paintings adorned the walls,
An upright piano festooned with music pamphlets
Mutti was a great pianist, she even sang,
And dad, a physician, a skin specialist
Enjoyed a large, well-earned practice.
"My room," Lieselotte half dreamt and recalled,
"Had my own wardrobe, a small bookcase,
A wonderfull collection of dolls
A clown picture on the wall.
And even a large dollhouse that Mutti and Vati gave me at Chanukah.
During the holidays aunts and uncles would visit
And Ursula, my best friend (she wasn't Jewish)
Would laugh and make up droll stories. But all that was before!"
The clatter of the railroad wheels below ever moving.

One day Mutti said, "You must go to a Jewish day school,
That's a rule and new law.
Vati can't practice at the hospital anymore nor treat non-Jewish patients.
Not allowed to go to the Kino, the movies
To the childrens' matinee on Saturday,
Or play with the other kids outside.
Our maid Justine had to be let go."

Many friends left for the United States or Palestine,
Or South America - things were getting ugly.
The raucous preaching by Hitler or Goebbels, or Goering
Drowned out any privacy.
The clatter of the railroad wheels below ever moving.

One day, on short order: "Must sell everything
and meet at the Marketplace with one suitcase each."
They say the law is the law.
"Vati always taught me to be honest and obedient
And so I reluctantly went along.
Our apartment was auctioned off in one day
And now we were headed to the Ghetto in Warsaw,
Everywhere there was poverty, hunger, stern faces.
What did we do? We were all so innocent and overwrought.
The clatter of the railroad wheels below ever moving.

"Was it my fault that my parents were born Jewish
And taught me the ten commandments as best they could?
I must cover my ears", Lieselotte thought.
"I must close my eyes and think of good things,
Birthday parties, Friday evening dinner with the Sabbath candles,
Vacation at the Ostsee at Nordernei.
I must hope again for a festive meal."
But Lieselotte's short life, little did she know,
Was coming to an end. Would it be soon?
After weeks of starvation and deprivation, huddled in Warsaw,
The family was broken up.
The clatter of the railroad wheels below ever moving.

One day they were lined up again,
Suitcase filled with what was left.
And so now she is in the jammed cars of cattle wagons ready for,
Yes, ready for Auschwitz. So much prospect! So much hope!
All vanished under the voice of the Final Solution,
The extermination of all Jews.
The clatter of the railroad wheels below ever moving.

All I can say is, "Auf Wiedersehn, Lieselotte -
You and one and half million other innocent
Children; victims of a mad, prejudiced society.

The clatter of the railroad wheels ceased.

Dessert

Dessert comes in many forms
Many stages
The palate begs
Be it mousse or cake
Fruit ice cream that is fake
A tort or specially designed
Fruit so exotic you can eat it blind

Biscuits, baked Alaska
Frittatas or special pasta
A kiss, a hug so in-between
Sandwiched, spontaneous and clean

I like a candy bar
It titillates and fills me up by far
Licorice, mint chocolate
Heaved on to spell my fate

The best dessert
Although you might get hurt
Is a love potion, slow to sip
Awesome as it pours over tongue and lip

If you ever want to be real crazy
Contentious at dinner table lazy
Start with dessert
With second helping that's so neat

By this time if still appetite
Broke the tradition sometime alright is quite
Each morsel mouth bit at your leisure
A third desert an ample pleasure

Gold Country near Sonora, CA

EVAPORATE

The rapids tested

The silver torrent cascades between the
        Steep and narrow boulder

Now water slowly spreads over
          a slivery silver glistening lake

    The boat steers placid, easy to maneuver

        Heading majestically downstream
          to meet the wide,
              inviting
                    open-aired lake

        Only to evaporate, rekindle

                    With steaming grace

FLOWERS

The red, yellow blossoms
Bouquet, rich colored blooms
Visual blessings from nature's bosom
With perfume fragrance into the house
The world outside now so within
But lifeline cut, the stems suck water
The flowers, distant from sun's warmth soon fade
Will wilt and spoil, sadly to be discarded
But you and I outlast those flowers
Our memories latched to their sunshine state
So lucky; I'll bring you more flowers soon!
Another rainbow cascade
Fleeting, relish in their gratifying beauty
Before the exhilaration pales

DAILY TASK

Ever stop in the morning and ask
"What today, is my daily task?"
Guided by a bright and shining light
Can I bring it to you and make it right?

    What good feelings do appeal?
    Make you happy, make you heal?
    Where to tickle, goof and gaff
    Make you chuckle, make you laugh?

        When to hold out a helping hand
        Make you smile, to understand?
        Train, run, skip, exercise
        Jump high, walk far, brings great surprise?

Eat healthy, stay lean
Dress attractively, sharp and clean
What will this day for us all now bring
With joy lighthearted, hear the birds and insects sing?

    Where, from gray cells direct that flow
    I will, I shall help someone I know
    So up and on with living in today
    Let me be cautious and go my way

        Decisive, I'll not give up
        I'll persevere and reach the top
        It's here. It's great. It's fate.
        It's never, ever, never too late

They say the higher they are, the harder they fall, but some of us have artificial wings.

TIME

Youth, you see with open eyes the aged
Stooped, wrinkled as they shuffle by
So withered worn
No one can deny their tired eyes reflect
Feelings, passions much like yours
Of love, hope and envy
A life to understand
Digesting bombardment of daily avalanche of news
His membranes, pathos, feelings deep
Friendship, tenderness, hope
Prayer of loneliness
Exuberance is rare
So is depression
Dressing, eating, walking, pills, washroom
Unsure, suspicious, alert, bent head unsteady
Hold on to few material things, what's left
They mean less and less each day

Think, young one
Where is your priority?
See his wisdom between the crags
His stubbled face, weight of history behind
Your benefits and letdowns were his creation
What do you have?
He hasn't luck and
Time

Can you see yourself at 70 or 85?
No, neither could I
Yet I am still alive

Yesterday was important, but it's today that really counts.

BANANA

A banana with its soft white shape
Is slightly inviting - more so for an ape
It's fresh and fulfilling
No dark spots, no mess, no juices spilling
Peel it, eat it, it's soft, not tough
Thank you! One banana at a time is enough.

BELIEVE

A touch of talent, if you believe
You will be gratified and soon receive
It takes some doing
Wooing, cooing
Energy to burn
Plan carefully your goal and learn
A bit of effort brings results
The deed accelerates the heart and pulse.

So within your limitations,
Thrust forth resolute with patience
Get off your butt and see, smell, partake
Like a morsel from a birthday cake
Taste each grand moment
Making effort you'll not resent

Your world may seem grim, yet is so gentle, so great
Go do it! Get up and move for heaven's sake!
Wait not for Monday or a blue moon,

Go start, right now, it's not too soon!

It's your life
Do what you choose
Some work hard while others snooze
Some are creative all the time
Others wasted their life of prime
So live and laugh and wonder
We all end up six feet under

"JUST FOR TODAY" *Daily Affirmations*

If you are a bit down, slightly depressed, as all of us are at times, try to recharge your personal battery! I share these insightful affirmations from others before me…

1. Just for today I will be happy. Happiness comes from within; it is not dependent on external influences.
2. Just for today I will try to adjust myself for what is, and not try to adjust everything to my own desires. I will take my luck as it comes and adjust accordingly.
3. Just for today I will take care of my body, I will exercise it, care for it, not abuse it. If I'm overweight or have a weakness, I will eat healthily.
4. Just for today I will strengthen my mind. I will learn something useful, not waste time. I will read, research, revise: something that takes thought and concentration to exercise my brain.
5. Just for today I will exercise my soul and do someone a good turn without taking credit. I will not dwell on negative thoughts, but on the beauty of nature, love and happiness.
6. Just for today I will be agreeable. I will dress with pride and groom myself. I will talk gently, act courteously, give praise readily, and not criticize. I will not find fault with anything and not try to regulate nor improve anyone. I will look for the good in everyone.
7. Just for today I will have a program. I will write down what I plan to achieve. I may not get to it all, but at least it is written down. This will eliminate two concerns; hurry and indecision. Just for today I will not try to tackle all my life problems at once. I will not plan far-reaching goals that will overwhelm me for a lifetime.
8. Just for today I will take time out for myself, even if it's only a half hour or so. I will relax, think and get a better perspective on my life.
9. Just for today I will be unafraid. I will not be scared, I will enjoy what is beautiful, to love and know that those that I love, love me.
10. Just for today I will do what is right and take responsibility for my actions. I will correct those things I can correct and accept those I cannot.

Based on Dale Carnegie's 1948 book: "How to Stop Worrying and Start Living," pp.112-113 It is called JUST FOR TODAY. Similar stuff was in "Dear Abby," January, 2009.

DRUGS AND ALCOHOL

Dare read this and save yourself and others! It's never too late!

He is only seventeen and he is almost past hope. This dear close relative, now a lousy student, is an addict. Unless someone intercedes, helps him, he will end up a vegetable. Does he know what will happen if he goes to prison? He will be marked for life. He will lose the right to vote, ruin his career path. He may become a homeless person - lost and eventually living off the street.

"Visual x-rays and other evidence have shown that excessive drug use damages your brain permanently. It will make you a slave to your addiction". You may even become a drug dealer, risking your life and negatively affecting everyone around you.

"Come on take some, smoke some, it will make you feel good," is a common peer-pressure invitation. "Go on, just try it. Your parents won't know. Look, we all have a great time. Take some!"
You know that drugs damage your body, especially your most precious brain, often permanently. You are a good person, but once under the influence anything destructive can happen. Driving under the influence has killed many innocents. You will lose your friends. Adults tell you: "Just say NO!" but that is not easy at times. You need the self control and willpower to refuse confidently and firmly. Only your inner strength and sensibility will prevent you from starting in the first place.

If you need help from family, school, support groups, speak up! After all, it's your precious life. Your family, your friends, those who love you, can get you help if you ask. They too are pained, and hurt badly. Next time at a party say courteously, "NO, I don't do that, thanks". Reject overtures to smoke swallow unknown pills, do coke other drugs. It can be and often is deadly. You have so much to look forward to in life, don't throw it away.

Have the guts to stand up to yourself, keep active. You can do it. Again, I ask you, I beg you - do not be a looser. Learn to politely say NO, or if hooked GET HELP.

My relative, together with tens of thousands is in prison NOW, a felon for life.

DISTRACTIONS

No more need to use our brain
Just rely on Google once again
Who needs to add numbers in one's head
Computer's easier, and correct instead

If I seek facts and faces
Computer in all places
Answer most questions in my scholarship
Just Google the answer - what a trip

Then why retain rote history facts
Leave my brain, please let it lax
Or theorems, algebraic rhythm
Or the affect of light on a prism?

At school friends' faces frame my mind
Attracts, distracts I may as well be blind
The essay homework - can't they ration?
Does all have to be a dissertation?

In morn and night I exercise
My body muscles a tough surprise
Do I have to keep up with girls and guys?
I hate to be cut down to size!

Why, oh why not sleep in late
Why clean my room or challenge fate?
I gobble down my food with speed
Try to keep clothes so clean and neat

Another party; must bring a gift
What to buy? Few bucks and thrift
Play iPods, joke and tease
Let me have fun and meet someone, please

POWER OF WORDS

Words are simply not enough
Each letter, each vowel, each invitation
Creeps on flowing, weaving sound waves
Audible the letter, the word, the thought
Jumps from end to end

Overwhelming, sound silent, smooth
Deafening
Staccato, halting
Sometimes singing
This supposed language we all speak
What if they all babble Greek?

Words in a sentence linked
The impending power of each thought
Transmitted and received
Cannot be bought

No man is an island unto himself
Words flow physically
So sincere a request
Come read with me
Telegraphed special
Hit the fuming bone
Of curiosity and atonement
Forgive, wish, praise
Is the child's tantrum any clearer
Than a grown up's?

Are you listening?

He could stand up to anything
Until he broke his leg
And with crutches he has more respect
For his body and the world

A NEW YEAR WISH

We each make our own bed
And make effort to be fed
I wish upon you a good year
Good health and such, my dear
For self-contentment - self satisfaction
Rewards for valor and good action
Good friends and health
Are really your greatest treasure and wealth

LET ME IN

My ego feeds the urge to write
Expand my being, day and night
Share some wisdom and inner thought
My soul never sold and never bought
I pour out treasure troves within
I feel you close
just
let
me
in

**I wish and hope for you the best
It's up to you to do the rest.**

*For more titles by Arthur Weil, please see page 3
or visit www.poetrypearls.com*